THE GIRL WHO
Asked for Presents

WRITTEN BY DANIELLE DEPRATT KOELBL

ILLUSTRATED BY ERIN BONHAM

SUPPORT AUTHORS TAYLOR AND ALEX KOELBL
EDITED BY LAURA JOECKEL

There once was a girl who always asked for presents. No matter how many toys she had or whether she was behaving good or bad, the girl always asked for a present.

One day, the girl woke up, ran out of her

bedroom and said to her parents,

"I WANT A PRESENT!"

Much to the girl's surprise, near her feet

there was the most beautifully wrapped

present she had ever seen. It was wrapped

in pink paper with a bow and sparkly ribbon.

The girl ripped open the pink paper

and tore off the bow and ribbon. When

she took off the top of the box and

looked inside, she found...

...a rock.

"This is NOT a present!" screamed the girl.

"Yes, it is," said her parents.

"No, it is not! This is a rock!" she insisted.

"A rock is a present. You can do many things with a rock. You can paint it, put papers under it..." began her parents.

The girl stormed off angrily,

leaving her present behind.

The next morning, the girl woke up,

ran to her parents and demanded,

"I WANT A PRESENT!"

Much to the girl's surprise, near her

feet was a long rectangular box. It was

wrapped in turquoise sparkle paper

with a ribbon and bow.

With a huge smile on her face the girl ripped

through the paper. When she opened the top

of the box and looked inside, she found…

…a rubber band.

"This is NOT a present!" screamed the girl.

"Yes, it is," said her parents.

"No, it is not! This is a rubber band!" she insisted.

"A rubber band is a present. You can do many

things with it. You can tie your hair into a ponytail,

make a bracelet…" her parents began.

The girl stormed off angrily,

leaving her present behind.

The next morning, the girl woke up,

ran to her parents and demanded,

"I WANT A PRESENT!"

Much to the girl's surprise, near her

feet was the largest present she had

ever seen. It was wrapped in silver

unicorn paper and a bright pink bow.

With a huge smile on her face, the girl ripped

through the paper. When she opened the top

of the box and looked inside, she found...

...a single tissue.

"This is NOT a present!" screamed the girl.

Before her parents could say anything, the

girl started to cry. She was so frustrated

and upset. Her parents took one look at

the tears rolling down her face and

handed her the tissue.

The girl walked away with her head hung low. She walked over to her play area, sat down and looked at her dolls. It had been a while since she played with her dolls. She then looked over at a tea set that she had never used. In that moment she decided her dolls should have a tea party.

She would be the hostess.

This is fun!

Days went by and the girl continued to create

new ways to play with her toys, until one day

she found a purple present sitting on the floor

of her playroom.

"Mom, can I open that purple present? I'm

going to make a castle with the box," she said.

Her parents smiled and nodded.

The girl tore off the ribbon and

opened the box.

There was nothing in it.

The girl smiled and said...

The girl collected her rock, rubber band,

and tissue and created a castle using the

empty purple box.

The parents smiled. Their daughter realized she already had everything she needed to be happy and that there are many ways to have fun with an empty "present" box.

Made in the USA
San Bernardino, CA
13 December 2018